I Am Loved
Meditating on the Scriptures

By Linda Patarello

I Am Loved
ISBN: 978-0-9896919-6-3

Editor: Daphne Parsekian

Published by Orion Productions, LLC.
P.O. Box 51194
Colorado Springs, CO 80949
Orionproductions.tv

These small books with scriptures that fit each theme are meant to help you learn how to meditate. Each scripture has my own meditative thoughts that follow. This will help you understand the thought flow that can happen when you think on God's Word. As you begin to think and ponder on God's word for yourself, you will find more revelation in the Scriptures that the Holy Spirit will reveal to you personally. I encourage you to read my initial book, How to Meditate on the Living Word. That will explain in more detail the process of meditation.

For now, I will simply state some scriptures that explain the importance of meditating and renewing your mind on the Holy Scriptures—two from the Old Testament and one from the New Testament.

"But his delight is in the law of the LORD; and in his law doth he meditate day and night. And he shall be like a tree planted by the rivers of water, that bringeth forth his fruit in his season; his leaf also shall not wither; and whatsoever he doeth shall prosper."

Psalm 1:2–3

"My son, attend to my words; incline thine ear unto my sayings. Let them not depart from thine eyes; keep them in the midst of thine heart. For they are life unto those that find them, and health to all their flesh."

Proverbs 4:20–22

"I beseech you therefore, brethren, by the mercies of God, that ye present your bodies a living sacrifice, holy, acceptable unto God, which is your reasonable service. And be not conformed to this world: but be ye transformed by the renewing of your mind, that ye may prove what is that good, and acceptable, and perfect, will of God."

Romans 12:1–2

It is not a waste of time to put your thoughts and your mind on God's Word—quite the opposite. You will be doing well for yourself, your body, your mind, and your future. It is rather a waste of time to worry and to only see and think on the problem or to dwell on the hopeless circumstances. Now, that really is a waste of time and can only bring death.

You can choose to make a new habit. And when you keep your thoughts on His Word, eventually it will come out of your mouth, and you will reap the benefits of it. You will have more peace, better health, and much more positive thoughts, full of life. You will experience this as you give yourself to thinking on the Scriptures. Don't take my word for it; put it to the test for yourself! Come on now, and let us meditate together. Once you begin to understand how, you can do it for yourself. I only want to simply show you how it is done.

"We love because he first loved us…"

1 John 4:16–21

He began to pursue you. It was His idea first. It was His idea to create you and His idea to love and chase you. When we know God loves us, a security comes over us. We are loved. A peace enters our hearts. Someone has pursued us. Someone loves us. This will cause a joy to rise up in us, where we will overflow and want to share His love with others.

"Because the love of God is shed abroad in our hearts by the Holy Ghost which is given to us."

Romans 5:5

Amplified:

"For God's love has been poured out in our hearts through the Holy Spirit Who has been given to us."

The Holy Spirit is God's gift to us and is a blessing to us in so many ways. One of these blessings is that the love of God has been poured into your heart. Sometimes a person can say, "I don't think I can love. It's too hard to love people that are mean." But really, God's love is in us through the Holy Spirit. We have His love. It is in us to partake of. You have all the love you need, for you and for others. So now, walk in it by faith. Begin to use it like you have it.

"Love never fails."

1 Corinthians 13:8

What the world needs now is love, but not just any love: the love of God as He gave His precious, only Son. Jesus gave Himself. He poured out His life, His love. Love restores and heals. When you encounter hard-to-love people, remember that the right way to treat them is with the love of God, and that love will not fail. You can also look at it another way; God loves you and will never fail. He will never stop loving you. His love will never fail. You can meditate on these words forever and each time you will see something new because His Words are alive.

"Yet the Lord will command his lovingkindness in the day time, and in the night his song shall be with me, and my prayer unto the God of my life."

Psalm 42:8

Other Bible versions say, "By day the LORD directs his love." Sometimes we have our minds on problems or the cares of this world and we miss looking at the good that God has done. This says "by day" which means every day.

"Follow the way of love."

1 Corinthians 14:1

7

This is the road we are supposed to take. We follow this way. This is actually a narrow way. Matthew 7:14 says, "Narrow is the way, which leadeth unto life, and few there be that find it." The way to life is through the love of God. As we love, we will find more life. There will be more peace. The way of love, remember, is a choice, not a feeling. We choose each day to love. We bite our tongue to keep out of trouble. It pleases God because that is how He loves. Do as your Father does.

"Thou shewest lovingkindness unto thousands…"

Jeremiah 32:18

God gets such a bad reputation sometimes; Satan spreads the lie that He is cruel and does evil acts. This scripture explains totally the opposite. He shows kindness because of His love; not just to a few but to thousands. The motive behind it in His heart is because He dearly loves you. He is the one who is full of compassion. He doesn't look at how imperfect you are; He wants to show kindness because He loves with an unconditional love, not a keeping score kind of love—you do good for me, then I'll love you. No. He spreads His love—just because.

"Fear not: for I have redeemed thee, I have called thee by thy name; thou art mine."

Isaiah 43:1

I used to read this in such a negative way due to not knowing the love of God; I thought He wanted to own me, to take my life from me and make me do things I didn't want to, like travel to Africa or the farthest places. I was very ignorant. It's not that way at all. Now I see this verse like this: When no one wants you, and they reject you, don't be afraid. I will never say that to you. I want you. I love you. I will be glad to call you my own. I will be glad to care for you. I know you. I will even call you by your name. You're not just a number; you're my precious creation.

"I, even I, am he that blotteth out thy transgressions for mine own sake, and will not remember thy sins."

Isaiah 43:25

Blot means to erase, to wipe away. God Himself has made a decision to erase your transgressions. He has decided to not even remember them. How many of us can do that? He does it for His own sake because He is a God of mercy and forgiveness. I also remember another scripture that goes with this: Psalm 103:12, which says, "As far as the east is from the west, so far hath he removed our transgressions from us." He's not looking for things that are wrong in you. He's looking for what's right. And that is what His son Jesus paid for. We stand in Jesus, and that is what God sees.

"Observe how Christ loved us. His love was not cautious but extravagant. He didn't love in order to get something from us but to give everything of himself to us. Love like that."

Ephesians 5:2, MSG

King James Version:

"And walk in love, as Christ also hath loved us, and hath given himself for us an offering and a sacrifice to God for a sweetsmelling savor."

Love, real agape love, does not even consider one's self. It risks being hurt, being taken for granted, and being taken advantage of. God's love doesn't play it safe. He gives and gives and gives, lavishly while throwing caution to the wind. This is the way He wants His children to live, pouring ourselves out just as Jesus did. Give and it shall be given unto you. The acts of Jesus were done with a right heart, which rose up high into heaven as a sweet smell to His Father.

"Let the beloved of the LORD rest secure in him, for he shields him all day long, and the one the LORD loves rests between his shoulders."

Deuteronomy 33:12

This verse was speaking of a son, Benjamin, but we can take it for us as well. You are the beloved of the Lord. And if the God of the universe sees you this way, as His beloved, then surely you should be secure in your heart. Why should I worry about anything? He loves me.

The security of His love will shield you all day long. The next part is very special: The one that the Lord loves rests between His shoulders. What is that? Between the shoulders is the heart, and you, dear one, are in His heart. When He thinks of you, it is with an endearing love not a sorry obligation. He does not regret one thing He suffered for you.

"Behold, what manner of love the Father hath bestowed upon us, that we should be called the sons of God:"

1 John 3:1

Behold means to look on, to gaze on. And what manner means what kind. What kind of love is this? The God of the universe is a Father indeed. And He has given us so much love that He has called us His sons, His children. He has made this possible by adopting us and accepting us as His own. How can we understand this? It is something too wonderful to grasp.

"Hereby perceive we the love of God, because he laid down his life for us: and we ought to lay our lives for the brethren."

1 John 3:16

This is how we see His love; this is how we understand it. Because He laid his life down for us, we can lay our life down for the brethren. To wrap your brain around this is astounding and takes tremendous humility. It takes a laying down of all pride and self will. We could only do this if we really had a revelation of His love for us. We can only do this through His strength and His power and grace. I can begin, in small ways, to put myself aside. The more I do this, the easier it will become. God's love puts others first and yourself last.

"For the Father himself loveth you, because ye have loved me, and have believed that I came out from God."

John 16:27

When someone is kind to my children and watches out for them, I appreciate it. I see this scripture as saying this as well. In other translations it states that the Father Himself tenderly loves you. First of all, He is a Father. God the Creator is a Father! And He's our Father. Because you believe in Jesus and love Jesus, the Father tenderly loves you. This type of love is called "phileo" in the Greek. It means to be a friend, to be fond of, and to have affection for.

"The LORD thy God in the midst of thee is mighty; he will save, he will rejoice over thee with joy; he will rest in his love, he will joy over thee with singing."

Zephaniah 3:17

New International Reader's Version:

"The LORD your God is with you. He is mighty enough to save you. He will take great delight in you. The quietness of his love will calm you down. He will sing with joy because of you."

I love the version above in the NIRV. I believe it is speaking of Jesus. It says in verse 15: "The LORD hath taken away thy judgments, he hath cast out thine enemy: the king of Israel, even the LORD, is in the midst of thee: thou shalt not see evil any more."

And now He is in the midst of you, if you are saved. He is mighty in you to save; He has become the curse for you and defeated the enemy. He has taken great delight in you and rejoiced in you. He has rescued and saved you because He loves you not because he had to. He chose to. He is excited about you. Some just can't see this, but it is here in the Word, and it is the truth. "He will rest in his love." I see this in my heart as twofold; when Christ finished His work, He went to heaven and sat at the right hand of God. Mark 16:19 says, "because of his love for us he finished the work and then rested." He did and completed the work.

The other idea is that when we are in the midst of a storm or overcome by turbulence and anxiety, doubt or fear, to be still…and let His love calm you. Picture the face of Jesus and let His love for you bring peace to your heart. Here is where I picture a wild stallion that only the master of that horse can tame and calm; only his own whisper into the horse's ear can bring him to a hushed calm.

"Can a mother forget the baby at her breast and have no compassion on the child she has borne? Though she may forget, I will not forget you! See, I have engraved you on the palms of my hands: your walls are ever before me."

Isaiah 49:15–16

If only the world were full of good mothers. We know that the fact is that this is not so, and it is a shame, but one thing we can be sure of is this: God the Father will never forget you. God is your Father, and He will always have compassion on you, for you are His child. A good father loves His kids and has mercy on them. Why, He even says, "See." See and look at His hands. Use your imagination and picture them. He says to you that He has engraved you on the palms of His hands. Sweethearts engrave and carve their names on a tree, hoping it will be there for life. They are telling each other, and the world, that they belong together, that they love each other. This reminds me of the holes in the hands of Jesus. His nail-scarred hands don't remind Him of the terrible pain He suffered. They remind Him of His love for you and how precious you are to Him.

Jesus is God come in the flesh. Your walls are ever before Him. Yes, this is speaking of the walls of

Jerusalem. But it is also speaking of us. Now let's think about this; walls are for protection. Now that we are in Christ, He is our protection; He is our shepherd.

"And call no man your father upon the earth: for one is your father, which is in heaven."

Matthew 23:9

Just as there are good and bad mothers, the same is true with fathers. We are all human, and if people did not grow up knowing and learning about God and His Word, they only know the ways of the world. However, regardless of good or bad, kind or mean, we must look to God as our real Father. The fact that He is a Father is amazing. The fact that He wants to be our Father is even more amazing. This means we have a family. A real family. One day we will see Him face to face. But for now, yes, you can enjoy Him, for He lives in you. He hears you and sees you, and if you listen to His still small voice, you will hear Him.

"Mercy triumphs over judgment."

James 2:13, NIV

Message:

"Kind mercy wins over harsh judgment every time." Wherever you look in this world there is judgment and pointing fingers. The world seems to enjoy and even be entertained by people falling and making mistakes. There are talk shows, sitcoms, reality shows, and magazines full of gossip proclaiming "Look who fell today." This all comes from Satan. He criticizes. He is the god of this world. He accuses the Christian and condemns us with constant guilt.

If you remember, wherever Jesus went on the earth, people would say, "Have mercy on me." They knew He had and showed mercy, for He showed love; He healed and delivered. This is our kingdom; this is where we need to live. Through the mercy of God, Jesus overcame judgment. In fact, He triumphed over judgment.

"I will never leave thee, nor forsake thee. So that we may boldly say, The Lord is my helper, and I will not fear what man shall do unto me."

Hebrews 13:5–6

Amplified:

"For He [God] Himself has said, I will not in any way fail you nor give you up nor leave you without support. [I will] not, [I will] not, [I will] not in any degree leave you helpless nor forsake nor let [you] down (relax My hold on you)! [Assuredly not!] So we take comfort and are encouraged and confidently and boldly say, The Lord is my Helper; I will not be seized with alarm [I will not fear or dread or be terrified]. What can man do to me?"

One of the main lies that the devil shouts to us is that we are alone. No one loves us. God has left us. These are out and out lies from Satan. Remember, he is the father of lies. This is a great scripture to memorize and meditate on often so that when a trial comes, one of the first things you can tell yourself is "I'm not alone. God is with me and for me." People may give up on you because they are human; they may not know the unconditional love of God. Friends will leave you and not support you. Spouses may leave. Parents may leave. But God is perfect. God is love. He never changes, and He is the biggest promise keeper in the universe. He will never let go of you. He loves watching over you. Believe His Word!

"For the mountains shall depart, and the hills be removed; but my kindness shall not depart from thee, neither shall the covenant of my peace be removed, saith the LORD that hath mercy on thee."

Isaiah 54:10

Amplified:

"For though the mountains should depart and the hills be shaken or removed, yet my love and kindness shall not depart from you, nor shall My covenant of peace and completeness be removed, says the Lord, Who has compassion on you."

Message:

"For even if the mountains walk away and the hills fall to pieces, my love won't walk away from you, my covenant commitment of peace won't fall apart. The GOD who has compassion on you says so."

When we read about mountains shaking and hills being removed, this is speaking about our crazy, overwhelming circumstances. They are always changing. We can never count on them staying the same. In fact, all the things your eyes see in the physical realm are subject to change. Don't hold onto them. They will let you down. His love for you will never end. Nothing can change how He feels about you. Nothing you can do will stop Him from loving you. Because of the covenant that Jesus made on our behalf with God, all this is so. This covenant is unbreakable; it is sure. How can God break an agreement with Himself? This is a God of compassion we are speaking about. And it is God Himself who is stating this. These words are coming out of His own mouth. Because of Jesus you have everlasting peace with God.

"For God so loved the world that he gave his only begotten Son, that whosoever believeth in him should not perish, but have everlasting life."

John 3:16

Amplified:

"For God so greatly loved and dearly prized the world, that he [even] gave up His only begotten (unique) Son, so that whoever believes in (trusts in, clings to, relies on) Him shall not perish (come to destruction, be lost) but have eternal (everlasting) life."

Sometimes we can overlook such a famous scripture. You've heard it tons of times before. I challenge you to look with new eyes. God is not cruel. God does not play games with people's lives. God is love. This verse does not say God loves the world. It says He SO loved the world. That little tiny word makes a difference. This means "very much"—so much that He did something about it. But wait. It says He loved the world. Who does this include? Does it leave anyone out? Not one.

Which one of us would give our child that we treasure for anyone else? This is how vast God's love is. Who can comprehend this kind of love that is free to all but costs the giver everything? He is saying, if you believe in my Son, you will never perish, but have everlasting life.

God was willing to save us from our destruction. No one else could save us. We could not save ourselves even. Oh the love of God, what a beautiful thing it is. When we have Jesus living in us, we have His love living in us as well. This means we can love this same way if we give ourselves to it. Surrender to His love and give up your will and your selfishness. To live and stay in this mind of love is what true life is all about. It is the highest life there is.

"Love is patient, love is kind. It does not envy, it does not boast, it is not proud. It does not dishonor others, it is not self-seeking, it is not easily angered, it keeps no record of wrongs. Love does not delight in evil but rejoices with the truth. It always protects, always trusts, always hopes, always perseveres. Love never fails."

1 Corinthians 13:4–8 (NIV)

This is the God kind of love. This is God's character. This is how God loves you and me and all the world. Let's read it as so:

God is patient with me. He is kind with me. He does not envy. He doesn't brag, and He isn't full of pride. God does not dishonor me or others. He is not self seeking; He is not easily angered. God keeps no record of wrongs. He doesn't focus on and remind me of my mistakes. God does not delight in evil or when bad things happen to me, but He rejoices with the truth. He always protects me, always trusts me, always hopes in me, and always perseveres. He is my biggest cheerleader. His love for me never fails.

"How excellent is thy lovingkindness, O God! therefore the children of men put their trust under the shadow of thy wings. They shall be abundantly satisfied with the fatness of thy house; and thou shalt make them drink of the river of thy pleasures. For with thee is the fountain of life: in thy light shall we see light. O continue thy lovingkindness unto them that know thee; and thy righteousness to the upright in heart."

Psalm 36:7–10

The love of God is so great! We as His children can come and hide under the shadow of His wings. We can trust Him and His protection and provision because we know He loves us. We are confident in that love. We come into His presence to worship, and we come expecting because we trust Him. We know we will walk away full. We will be nourished, fed, refreshed, and overflowing when we come into His presence. We won't be just satisfied. We are sure to be abundantly satisfied. He will make us drink of the river of His pleasures. He has nothing but life and goodness to give.

With Him is the fountain of life! Picture yourself near a beautiful fountain. Imagine the spray of it on you, so refreshing. You can come into His presence any time you want to. Because of Jesus, you now have an open invitation. We are the ones that can stray away from Him. He never leaves or strays away from us. We will see His light as we walk in that light. 1 John 2:10–11 says that when you walk in God's love, you are walking in the light. Because we know Him, He will continue His lovingkindness towards us.

"God is love."

1 John 4:8

19

Even though this is a very short phrase, as you get more familiar with meditating on the Scriptures and are led by the Holy Spirit, you will find that this phrase can speak volumes. It ties in with so many other scriptures. This verse could have said God is joy, or God is peace. We know He has these qualities, but it doesn't say that. It says God is love. He is not hate. He is not cruel. He is full of mercy and forgiveness. These stem from His love. Peace and joy stem from His love. If He doesn't change, like it says in James 1:17, then He has always been love. This means that love always was. That love created the earth. It was love that created Adam. And the motivation to make man was love.

"God is love; and he that dwelleth in love dwelleth in God, and God in him."

1 John 4:16

A child learns what they live with from their parents. Good habits and bad habits. In this case, there are no bad habits with God. He is love. And as we follow him and His ways, we will be love. We must give ourselves to this love. We surrender to it. It is a choice, not a feeling. And notice the word "dwell." This means to live, to stay. So in other words, you don't come to it when it's convenient or when you're feeling compassionate and merciful. You stay. You stay and live there through thick and through thin. This is your home, for this is God's home. People will see this love that is so fantastically different from anything else they've seen. The world has nothing like it and never will.

"According as he has chosen us in him before the foundation of the world, that we should be holy and without blame before him in love."

Ephesians 1:4

This verse declares so much; it can never be described in a simple paragraph. You and I were a thought and a picture in His mind before He even created the world. Not only that, but He saw your whole life all at once. He planned your life and a good life at that (Jer. 29:11). He chose us.

"But God, who is rich in mercy, for his great love wherewith he loved us."

Ephesians 2:4

Who can you say of anyone on this earth, "Ah, they are rich in mercy"? Maybe some mature Christians will have much mercy as they choose to live there. But even they are only human. Yes, we have Christ living in us, but we still live in this fleshly body, and we still get physically tired. But God never gets tired, never sleeps, and never grows weary. He is truly rich in mercy and compassion, forgiveness and goodness. We see people who are rich in bank accounts. God is rich in mercy, meaning He has plenty of mercy to go around; He will never run out. He has so much that in His great love, He chose to love you and me.

'Who shall separate us from the love of Christ? shall tribulation, or distress, or persecution, or famine, or nakedness, or peril, or sword?"

Romans 8:35

Nothing on this earth, no matter how bad or how extreme, that we go through can ever stop His love to us.

This is what He does. He loves, He is love, and He will keep loving throughout eternity. Christ loved us in our wretched sin. He died for us when we were at our worst. And even when you get saved and slip into sin, still you cannot stop Him from loving you. You may hide in your guilt and choose not to run to Him, but His arms are always open, for He has paid for your forgiveness. Dare to run into the arms of His never ending love.

"Nay, in all these things we are more than conquerors through him that loved us."

Romans 8:37

In all these things, meaning tribulation, distress, persecution, famine, nakedness, peril, sword, etc., we still come out on top. He defeated sin, defeated Satan. Jesus is the victor, and we get to partake in that victory. In fact, we are more than conquerors because we didn't have to do a thing except believe and receive him as our Lord and Savior. He did the work, and He causes us to reap the benefits! He is so good and so loving to us even when we surely didn't deserve it.

"I in them, and thou in me, that they may be made perfect in one; and that the world may know that thou hast sent me, and hast loved them, as thou hast loved me."

John 17:23

His prayer to His Father and our Father is that we should be one in Him and in each other. One. No divisions, no unforgiveness. One body. Nourishing and nurturing each other, preferring one another. There should be such a difference in us that the world will see it and that they will know clearly that we are different.

They should know that God the Father loves us and loved Jesus. Sometimes we walk around not realizing that Christ really lives in us. We forget about that. He sees what we see, feels what we feel, and hears what we hear, and He wants us to become aware of that. He wants us to become aware of His deep love for us; that it would envelope us so much that we would walk in that same love for each other.

"Shew thy marvellous lovingkindness, O thou that savest by thy right hand them which put their trust in thee from those that rise up against them."

Psalm 17:7

When He shows up in your life and rescues you or protects and saves you from evil situations, you can be sure that He is showing His marvelous lovingkindness. He is doing it because He loves you. He is doing this because you are trusting Him. He loves when His kids trust Him. He loves to show forth His strength like a good Father. You can picture a dad coming to his child's school and showing up to face the bully that picked on his child. He is glad to protect and defend. God is a strong, loving Father, and He is no different; in fact, He is even more protective.

"Remember, O LORD, thy tender mercies and thy lovingkindnesses; for they have been ever of old."

Psalm 25:6

The tender mercies and lovingkindness of God have always been. To us they are from old, but they actually have always been in existence because God has always been. He is the Alpha and Omega, the great I

AM. He will never run out. We will be experiencing his lovingkindness throughout time and for all eternity. We will be amazed over and over again at how great His love is toward us.

"For thy lovingkindness is before mine eyes: and I have walked in thy truth."

Psalm 26:3

Sometimes we can wake up on the wrong side of the bed and miss seeing His goodness throughout the day. It's much easier for people to see the negative and the things that are not perfect—the things that are not done—than to see the good side. You must get in the habit of opening your eyes and looking on the good. Open your eyes and see his lovingkindness; see even the little blessings that come your way throughout your days. You walk outside and hear a bird singing a simple song. Don't take things for granted. Think about it. That bird is actually singing praises to God, for that is how God made him. Let everything that hath breath praise the Lord, the psalmist wrote. Watch for His lovingkindness. When you walk in His truth and keep His truth in your mind, you will see His lovingkindness.

"I have not concealed thy lovingkindness and thy truth from the great congregation."

Psalm 40:10

The world needs to know this great loving God. The Church needs to know of His lovingkindness. We can plant seeds and share of His goodness. Sometimes their eyes can also be closed to seeing His love. God can use us to share with them; we must not hide it and keep it all to ourselves. The world is starving for love. Spread the good news.

"Withhold not thou thy tender mercies from me, O LORD: let thy lovingkindness and thy truth continually preserve me."

Psalm 40:11

We can surely see in the New Testament that He has not withheld from us. He has given us everything that pertains to life and godliness (1 Peter 1:3). He has given us Jesus. His lovingkindness and His truth have been given freely to us. His Word sanctifies us (John 17:17). His Word washes over our minds as we give ourselves to it, renewing our thoughts. His word preserves us continually.

"Because thy lovingkindness is better than life, my lips shall praise thee."

Psalm 63:3

Life is good in itself, but it does not compare to the life we can have with the Lord. He is the source of our life and the reason we sing—the reason we love and laugh. His lovingkindness is so sweet that it is better than life. Life will one day end on this earth, and He will create a new heaven and a new earth. But his lovingkindness will never end; it will always be. Because He has given you and me new life, we will always be. Forever my lips shall praise Him for all the kindness He has shown to me. He didn't have to give me eternal life, but He did. And even more, He has welcomed us to live with Him as His children forever. My lips shall praise You my God, my Father, my Jesus, my Savior!

"Also I will make him my firstborn, higher than the kings of the earth. My mercy will I keep for him for evermore, and my covenant shall stand fast with him. His seed also will I make to endure for ever, and his throne as the days of heaven."

Psalm 89:27–29

Jesus is God come in the flesh. Romans 8:11 speaks of how the Spirit raised Christ from the dead. He is higher than any king on the earth; He is the King of kings and the Lord of Lords. Every benefit that Jesus has been given we can partake of if we are in Him. God said He will keep His mercy for him forevermore, and the same goes for us in Christ. God made a covenant with Jesus that will last forever. It will never break. We can always enjoy this covenant of peace; it will never end. How can it end if Jesus made the covenant with God? Perfect plus perfect equals perfect. His seed is speaking of us. That we could live forever and ever in peace with the Father Almighty, with Jesus and the Holy Spirit, is amazing. We are blessed beyond measure.

"To shew forth thy lovingkindness in the morning, and thy faithfulness every night."

Psalm 92:2

If we realize it and open our eyes to it, we can see His lovingkindness every morning. When the sun comes up and shines on everything and everyone, that alone is a blessing. It's the time when all creation begins to sing and rejoice. I remember one morning sitting in my backyard drinking my coffee and meditating on Scripture, worshiping Jesus, and I looked up and sat still. All of a sudden I became aware of my surroundings, which were very busy: bees buzzing back and forth; humming birds stopping to flutter on a flower; dragonflies flying above; mixed with grasshoppers and butterflies. If you think about it, yes, they are busy working on finding food, but they are also praising their Creator because they are doing what they were designed to do. A new day equals new mercies. And by the end of the day, after you have seen your Father answering prayers and using you to be a blessing, you can thank Him at night for His faithfulness.

"Who redeemeth thy life from destruction; who crowneth thee with lovingkindness and tender mercies;"

Psalm 103:4

I believe that when we get to heaven, we will hear and find out all of the many stories of where the Lord rescued and saved us from harm. He not only redeems us but He crowns us with lovingkindness. We did not deserve any kindness, but He did it anyway because of His great love.

"I will worship toward thy holy temple, and praise thy name for thy lovingkindness and for thy truth: for thou hast magnified thy word above all thy name."

Psalm 138:2

When I think about the words "toward thy holy temple," I am reminded that in the Old Testament, this is where God's presence was. But now, in the New Testament, through the finished work of Christ, His presence is in us every day and from now on and forever. I will worship Him anywhere, anytime. That it would give Him joy to be kind to us and that He loves to do this for

His children means He is such a good Father, a good God. I can worship Him for His truth, and we know that His truth is His word. His truth is full of life to us. His truth sets us free. In Psalm 107:20 it mentions that He sent His word and healed them. We know that His Word is Jesus. We also read that from John 1:14: And the Word was made flesh, and dwelt among us, and we beheld his glory.

It reminds me of Philippians 2:9–10, where it says God has highly exalted Him and given Him a name which is above every name. Jesus went to the lowest depths, and God then chose to exalt Him higher than any name.

"The LORD hath appeared of old unto me, saying, Yea, I have loved thee with an everlasting love: therefore with lovingkindness have I drawn thee."

Jeremiah 31:3

If the love of God is everlasting, that means it always was, even before we were and created. And His love is everlasting, meaning it will never end or even run out. His love for me is forever. He has drawn me with lovingkindness not cruelty or the pointing of the finger, telling me of all my mistakes and failures. Romans 2:4 says it's the goodness of God that leads men to repentance. When a person comes to us and points out our wrongs and tells us how to do it right, we are not encouraged but more likely pushed away. Yet when someone comes to you and points out your good points and compliments you with honesty and sincerity, you are blessed and want to go the extra mile for them. God is this way. Jesus didn't come to condemn the world but to save it.

"And I will betroth thee unto me for ever; yea, I will

betroth thee unto me in righteousness, and in judgment, and in lovingkindness, and in mercies."

Hosea 2:19

This verse also proves the one before it. He didn't woo us with cruelty and punishment or with manipulative control and anger. He wooed us with mercies and in righteousness. Jesus gave Himself for us, and He loved us first. He wants us. And He wants us for His own. He wanted to betroth us to Him forever. This relationship will always be new and never get old and worn out. He is a righteous, fair judge, full of forgiveness and mercy.

"I have heard your prayer and seen your tears." (NIV)

2 Kings 20:5

We sometimes, or I should say many times, think God has forgotten us. We see Him at times as far away and that He doesn't know what we are going through and couldn't possibly understand our circumstances. But that is wrong and actually a lie. He knows and sees everything. Nothing gets past our God. He does hear our prayers. He has seen every single one of your tears that you have cried in private, even when you thought no one cared.

"Thou tellest my wanderings: put thou my tears into thy bottle: are they not in thy book?"

Psalm 56:8

How much love and compassion does this God have? This Father of mercies and God of all comfort (2 Corinthian 1:3).

Think of all the tears you've ever cried throughout you entire life: when you were a baby and then a child; as you went through your school years; as you grew up and got married; as your life may have not turned out as you wanted it to or thought and planned it would. You may have had many disappointments in life. Things and people may have not been fair to you. But God your father saw it all. And He knew about every single one of your tears. This verse says He even saved them in His bottle. He cares more than you or I know. I believe when we get to heaven, we will be so surprised when we are able to see clearly for ourselves how much He cares for each one of us.

About the Author

Linda Patarello is a born again Christian, and graduate from Charis Bible College in Colorado Springs, Colorado. She currently lives there, and spends most of her time spreading the truth about God's Love from the written Word. Linda is a California native with broad experience in leading praise & worship and songwriting. She believes that the highest calling is to worship the "Giver of All Gifts." She also believes we are born to pursue a relationship with God the Father, Jesus Christ and the Holy Spirit, and to share it with others. Her vision is to help people find true love for the Word of God, and to uncover its precious truths that are waiting to be revealed.

For More Information or to Contact the Author, Please Write to:

Linda Patarello
P.O. Box 7964
Colorado Springs, CO 80933

www.Heartsower.com

Prayer of Salvation

There is nothing more fulfilling in life than knowing that God loves you. God has made, and continues to make His love known to us by having sent His only begotten son, Jesus Christ, to die on the cross as payment for our sins and the injustices done unto us.

Has anyone willingly given up their life in exchange for yours, so that you may live? Jesus did. "Greater love hath no man than this, that a man lay down his life for his friends" (Jn. 15:13). Notice, that Jesus said this *before* he went to the cross. He laid down His life for us because he saw you and I, his friends, benefiting from this act of love.

You were the joy that was set before Jesus. "For the joy that was set before him [he] endured the cross, despising the shame, and is set down at the right hand of the throne of God" (Heb. 12:2). Only a true, selfless friend could love like this. Would you like to know the One Who finds you valuable, Who truly loves you? If you would like to ask Jesus to be your friend and your Lord and Savior, you can ask Him today. You can use your own words or pray,

"Lord Jesus, I want to know you, I want to be your friend. I invite you into my life, so that I may know you more. Be my saving friend, Lord and Savior. I am sorry for all my sins and past mistakes. Thank you for forgiving me and loving me, in spite of my past. You are my friend, even when I have no one else. I want to receive everything you have for me, even your Holy Spirit. Take control of my life, and through my relationship with you, let it grow and mature, and become a light unto others. Thank you for freeing me from sin and darkness, and for putting me in right-standing with you forever. I am saved! Thank you, Jesus! Amen!

If you prayed this prayer for the first time in your life, we believe that you are born again! Find a good Bible-based church, and connect with other believers. Please share your testimony or visit us online:

http://www.orionproductions.tv/contact-us.html

You can write to us:

Orion Productions

PO Box 51194
Colorado Springs, CO 80949

Blessings to you! From our staff at Orion Productions.

To make known the stories and accounts of God's work in people's lives through multimedia products and services.

Our latest publishing information can be found by visiting our website at:

www.orionproductions.tv/publishing.html